S0-DXO-751

To: Charla
From: The Godfreys
1986

THE SHAPE OF POETRY

Keep a poem in your pocket
and a picture in your head,
and you'll never feel lonely
at night when you're in bed.

The little poem will sing to you;
the little picture will bring to you
a dozen dreams to dance to you
at night when you're in bed.

So—
Keep a picture in your pocket
and a poem in your head,
and you'll never feel lonely
at night when you're in bed.

—Beatrice Schenk de Regniers

illustrated by Lois Axeman

THE CHILD'S WORLD

ELGIN, ILLINOIS 60120

compiled by Evi Solomon

Distributed by Childrens Press, 1224 West Van Buren Street,
Chicago, Illinois 60607.

Library of Congress Cataloging in Publication Data

Main entry under title:

Holidays.

  (The Shape of poetry)
  Summary: A collection of poems about the year's
holidays, from New Year's Day to Christmas.
  1. Holidays—Juvenile poetry. 2. Children's
poetry, American. [1. Holidays—Poetry. 2. American
poetry—Collections] I. Axeman, Lois, ill. II. Series.
PS595.H6H64 1984   811'.008'033   84-9429
ISBN 0-89565-266-8

© 1984 The Child's World, Inc.
All rights reserved. Printed in U.S.A.

1 2 3 4 5 6 7 8 9 10 11 12 R 91 90 89 88 87 86 85 84

LAST night, while we were fast asleep,
  The old year went away.
It can't come back again because
  A new one's come to stay.

—*Rachel Field*

4

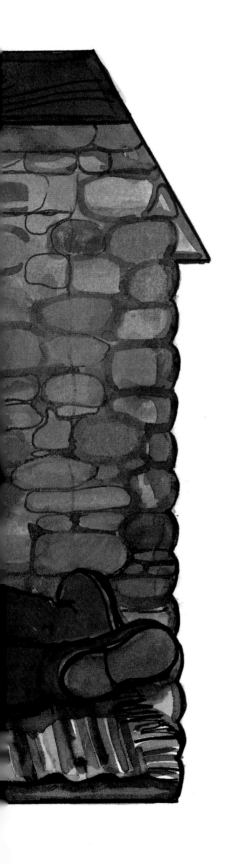

ABRAHAM LINCOLN
  lived long ago.
There were so many things
  he wanted to know,

That he lay on the floor
  and studied at night.
He read and did math
  in the dim firelight.

President Lincoln
  was called "Honest Abe."
He lived in the White House
  and helped free the slaves.

He was tall and kind
  our history books say,
We think of him each year
  on his special day.

                  —Colleen L. Reece

Do you love me or do you not?
You told me once but I forgot.

—Anonymous

A VALENTINE is fun to send.
I took one to my next-door friend.
I made it myself—with hearts and lace—
And wrote a special line.
I wrote it BIG. Here's what
It said: BE MY VALENTINE.

—Jane Buerger

HE fought for his country
   At Valley Forge.
His soldiers were hungry.
   So was George.

They were sick and freezing.
   So was he.
But they kept on fighting
   To make us free.

When the guns were quiet,
    And the war was won,
The soldiers marched home
    With Washington.

People laughed and shouted.
    They were no longer sad.
George Washington became president,
    The first one we had.

—Colleen L. Reece

IT ought to come in April,
or, better yet, in May,
when everything is green as green—
I mean St. Patrick's Day.

With still a week of winter,
this wearing of the green
seems rather out of season—
it's rushing things, I mean.

But maybe March *is* better
when all is done and said:
St. Patrick brings a promise,
a four-leaf-clover promise,
a green-all-over promise
of springtime just ahead!

—*Aileen Fisher*

ON EASTER morn at early dawn
    before the cocks were crowing,
I met a bobtail bunnykin
    and asked where he was going.
" 'Tis in the house and out the house
    a-tipsy, tipsy-toeing,

            'Tis round the house and 'bout the house
                a-lightly I am going."
            "But what is that of every hue
                you carry in your basket?"
            " 'Tis eggs of gold and eggs of blue;
                I wonder that you ask it.

'Tis chocolate eggs and bonbon eggs
   and eggs of red and gray,
For every child in every house
   on bonny Easter Day."
He perked his ears and winked his eye
   and twitched his little nose;

        He shook his tail — what tail he had —
           and stood up on his toes.
        "I must be gone before the sun;
           the east is growing gray.
        'Tis almost time for bells to chime."
           So he hippety-hopped away.

—Rowena Bennett   15

ON MOTHER'S Day we got up first,
so full of plans we almost burst.

We started breakfast right away
as our surprise for Mother's Day.

We picked some flowers, then hurried back
to make the coffee — rather black.

We wrapped our gifts and wrote a card
and boiled the eggs — a little hard.

And then we sang a serenade,
which burned the toast, I am afraid.

But Mother said, amidst our cheers,
"Oh, what a big surprise, my dears.
I've not had such a treat in years."
And she was smiling to her ears!

—*Aileen Fisher*

I'VE got a rocket
In my pocket,
I cannot stop to play.
Away it goes!
I've burnt my toes.
It's Independence Day.

—Unknown

18

JUST see those pinwheels whirling round
Spitting sparkles on the ground,
And watch that rocket whoosh so high,
Then turn to flowers in the sky —
Green and yellow, blue and red.
And look at *me* still not in bed!

Dorothy Aldis

19

ON HALLOWEEN my friends and I
Dress up in frightening clothes.
We each put on a funny face
With an e-nor-mous nose.

We ring our neighbors' doorbells,
And they get an awful fright
To see such scary creatures
Standing there at night!

—*Charlotte Yoder Cutler*

21

Mr. Macklin
takes his knife
and carves
the yellow
    pumpkin
        face.
Three holes bring
eyes and nose to life,
the mouth has
thirteen
    teeth
        in place.
Then Mr. Macklin
just for fun
transfers
the corncob
    pipe
        from his
wry mouth to Jack's,
and everyone
dies laughing!
O what
    fun
        it is. . .

till Mr. Macklin
draws the shade
and lights
the candle
   in Jack's
     skull.
Then all the inside
dark is made
as spooky
and
   as
     horrorful
as Halloween,
and creepy crawl
the shadows
on the
   toolhouse
     floor,
with Jack's face
dancing on the wall.
O Mr. Macklin!
Where's
   the
     door?

—David McCord

23

PEACE and Mercy and Jonathan,
And Patience (very small),
Stood by the table giving thanks
The first Thanksgiving of all.

Thankful they were their ship had come
Safely across the sea;
Thankful for hearth and home,
And kin and company.

They were glad of broth to go with their bread,
Glad their apples were round and red,
Glad of mayflowers they would bring
Out of the woods again next spring.

So Peace and Mercy and Jonathan,
And Patience (very small),
Stood up gratefully giving thanks
The first Thanksgiving of all.

—*Nancy Byrd Turner*

CHANUKAH, Chanukah!
What a holiday!
Candlelights burning bright.
Children play.

Chanukah, Chanukah!
Eight days full of fun!
Dreidel games near the flames
Warming everyone.

—*Karen Sussan*

ONE CHRISTMAS when Santa Claus
　Came to a certain house,
To fill the children's stockings there,
　He found a little mouse.

"A Merry Christmas, little friend,"
　Said Santa good and kind.

"The same to you, sir," said the mouse,
　"I thought you wouldn't mind,
If I should stay awake tonight
　And watch you for a while."

"You're very welcome, little mouse,"
　Said Santa, with a smile.

And then he filled the stockings up
　Before the mouse could wink—
From toe to top, from top to toe,
　There wasn't left a chink.

"Now they won't hold another thing,"
　Said Santa Claus with pride.
A twinkle came in Mouse's eyes,
　But humbly he replied:

"It's not polite to contradict—
    Your pardon I implore—
But in the fullest stocking there
    I could put one thing more."

"Oh, ho!" laughed Santa. "Silly mouse,
    Don't I know how to pack?
By filling stockings all these years
    I should have learned the knack."

And then he took the stocking down
    From where it hung so high,
And said, "Now put in one thing more,
    I give you leave to try."

The mousie chuckled to himself,
    And then he softly stole
Right to the stocking's crowded toe
    And gnawed a little hole!

"Now, if you please, good Santa Claus,
    I've put in one thing more,
For you will own that little hole
    Was not in there before."

How Santa Claus did laugh and laugh!
    And then he gaily spoke,
"Well, you shall have a Christmas cheese
    For that nice little joke!"

If you don't think this story is true,
    Why, I can show to you
The very stocking with the hole
    The little mouse gnawed through!

—Emilie Poulsson

"ARE the reindeer in the rain, dear?"
Asked Mrs. Santa Claus.
"No. I put them in the barn, dear,
To dry their little paws."

"Is the sleigh, sir, put away, sir,
In the barn beside the deer?"
"Yes. I'm going to get it ready
To use again next year."

"And the pack, dear, is it back, dear?"
"Yes. It's empty of its toys,
And tomorrow I'll start filling it,
For next year's girls and boys."

—*Rowena Bennett*

GOD bless the master of this house,
   The mistress also,
And all the little children
   That round the table go,
And all your kin and kinsmen
   That dwell both far and near;
I wish you a Merry Christmas
   And a Happy New Year.

—*Old Rhyme*

Grateful acknowledgement is made to the following for permission to reprint their copyrighted material.

"Keep a Poem in Your Pocket" (pg. 1) from SOMETHING SPECIAL, © 1958 by Beatrice Schenk deRegniers. Reprinted by permission of Harcourt Brace Jovanovich, Inc.

"New Year's Day" (pg. 4) from A LITTLE BOOK OF DAYS by Rachel Field. Copyright 1927 by Doubleday and Company, Inc. Reprinted by permission of Doubleday and Company, Inc., and World's Work Ltd.

"Wearing of the Green" (pg. 13) reprinted from HOLIDAY PROGRAMS FOR BOYS AND GIRLS, by Aileen Fisher. Copyright © 1953, 1970, 1980 by Aileen Fisher. Plays, Inc., Publishers, Boston, MA.

"Meeting the Easter Bunny" (pg. 14) from SONGS AROUND A TOADSTOOL TABLE by Rowena Bastin Bennett. Copyright © 1937 by Modern Curriculum Press. Used by permission of Modern Curriculum Press.

"On Mother's Day" (pg. 17) from SKIP AROUND THE YEAR by Aileen Fisher (T. Y. Crowell). Copyright © 1967 by Aileen Fisher. Reprinted by permission of Harper and Row, Publishers, Inc.

"Fourth of July Night" (pg. 19) by Dorothy Aldis. Reprinted by permission of G. P. Putnam's Sons from ALL TOGETHER, copyright 1925-1928, 1934, 1939, 1952; copyright renewed © 1953-1956, 1962, 1967, 1980 by Dorothy Aldis.

"Halloween Scare" (pg. 21) by Charlotte Yoder Cutler, from AWAY WE GO! 100 POEMS FOR THE VERY YOUNG. Copyright CHILDREN'S ACTIVITIES. Used by permission of Highlights for Children, Inc., Columbus, Ohio.

"Mr. Macklin's Jack o'Lantern" (pg. 22) from ONE AT A TIME by David McCord. Copyright 1952 by David McCord. First appeared in FAR AND FEW by David McCord. Used by permission of Little, Brown, and Company.

"First Thanksgiving of All" (pg. 24) by Nancy Byrd Turner from FAVORITE POEMS OLD AND NEW, published 1957 by Doubleday and Company. Copyright owned by Melvin Lee Steadman, Jr.

"Conversation Between Mr. and Mrs. Santa Claus" (pg. 30) by Rowena Bennett from JACK AND JILL. Copyright © 1947 by The Curtis Publishing Company. Used by permission of Kenneth C. Bennett, Jr.